YOUR KNOWLEDGE HA

Alrik Degenkolb

Social Feed Reader - Specification of a prototype

GRIN Publishing

Bibliographic information published by the German National Library:

The German National Library lists this publication in the National Bibliography; detailed bibliographic data are available on the Internet at http://dnb.dnb.de .

Imprint:

Copyright © 2009 GRIN Verlag GmbH
Print and binding: Books on Demand GmbH, Norderstedt Germany
ISBN: 978-3-640-38814-1

This book at GRIN:

http://www.grin.com/en/e-book/131750/social-feed-reader-specification-of-a-pro-totype

GRIN - Your knowledge has value

Since its foundation in 1998, GRIN has specialized in publishing academic texts by students, college teachers and other academics as e-book and printed book. The website www.grin.com is an ideal platform for presenting term papers, final papers, scientific essays, dissertations and specialist books.

TECHNISCHE UNIVERSITÄT CHEMNITZ
FACULTY OF BUSINESS

Chair of Business Information Systems II

Social Feed Reader:
Specification of a prototype

Author:	Alrik Degenkolb
Register:	2004
Field of study:	Business Information Systems
Date:	24/05/2009

Table of contents

List of figures

List of abbreviations

GUI	Graphical User Interface
HTML	Hypertext Markup Language
MCF	Meta Content Framework
PDA	Personal Digital Assistant
RDF	Resource Description Format
RSS	Really Simple Syndication
URI	Uniform Resource Identifier
XHTML	Extensible Hypertext Markup Language
XML	Extensible Markup Language
W3C	World Wide Web Consortium

Abstract

Management of information is gaining rising importance in knowledge intensive projects. Many information sources in the web provide feeds for easy accessibility. While there are a variety of software tools for personal feed consumption, collaborative approaches are still rare.

This research project focuses on the theoretical aspect of feeds and their technical background like Atom and RSS. Furthermore it gives an overview about the historical development and intention of feeds and how it is used today.

It also provides an overview about related research projects and existing tools. The paper concludes with an ideal social feed reader using common principles of social software, like tagging, social networking, social recommendation and microblogging.

1 INTRODUCTION

The access to the big bulk of information in the internet and also enterprise specific intranet has become more crucial. The borders between specialised and common knowledge are blurred. We are overstrained by the masses of emails, new Wikipedia entries, project timetable changes and updates on web pages.[1]
Nevertheless we have to keep track of the information flow in case something interesting comes along. The publications can be accessed via multiple devices like PDA's, cell phones, notebooks, as well as MP3 and video players. Furthermore software vendors are releasing new applications on mobile devices, news agencies are establishing new channels to access the newest content and normal internet users are shifting away from being content customers and become content publishers. Participation is the big challenge of the internet as a platform, named Web 2.0.[2]

The intention of this paper is the discourse about the basic technologies and related research projects as well as existing tools. The paper finishes with a blueprint of a nice-to-have feed reader facilitating co-operation in working groups.

2 TECHNOLOGIES AND TERMINOLOGY

2.1 FEEDS

Feeds, also known as web feeds or news feeds are publish-subscribe delivery vehicles to spread recently updated content to subscribers.
Technically feeds are data in a specific format, which is primarily not directly human-readable but can be interpreted and pre-processed by applications for the user to read. Feeds "[...] *are gaining wide acceptance with applications spanning information delivery, sensor monitoring, auction systems, and air traffic control"*.[3]

---

[1] Hoguhton-Jan, "Being Wired or Being Tired - 10 Ways to Cope with Information Overload."

[2] Alby, "Web 2.0. Konzepte, Anwendungen, Technologien", chap. 6.

[3] Liu, Ramasubramanian, and Sirer, "Client Behavior and Feed Characteristics of RSS, a Publish-Subscribe System for Web Micronews."

Little orange buttons labeled with XML, feed, RSS, Atom and further variants are available to represent the syndication – see figure one for an excerpt.

In comparison to email, syndication formats do not need any personal information from the user before subscribing or unsubscribing, in contrast to email newsletters.

figure 1: rss graphics in accordance to www.rss-specifications.com

2.2 REALLY SIMPLE SYNDICATION (RSS)

"RSS is a web content syndication format"[4].

This dialect of XML must be valid to the XML 1.0 specification of the World Wide Web Consortium (W3C). The current version of RSS is 2.0, but RSS 1.0 can still be found as an alternative. The abbreviation RSS represents either Really Simple Syndication or, out of date sometimes Rich Site Summary / RDF Site Summary. Software can be utilized to keep track of published content via the RSS format, so called 'aggregators' or 'feed readers'.

2.3 ATOM

"Atom is an XML-based document format that describes lists of related information known as 'feeds'. Feeds are composed of a number of items, known as 'entries', each with an extensible set of attached metadata."[5]

Atom has some crucial differences in comparison to RSS[6]:

- Atom contains a XML schema.
- RSS – elements can contain plaintext or HTML but it is not labeled, in contrast to Atom where elements can be used with plaintext , HTML or XHTML
- You can use relative URIs in an Atom document.
- In contrast to RSS, where the <description> element can contain a summary or the whole entry (which is very irritating due to a missing labeling mechanism), Atom utilizes a separate <summary> and <content> element to express the content.
- Each entry in an Atom – feed obtains a unique identifier.

---

[4] "RSS 2.0 Specification (RSS 2.0 at Harvard Law)."

[5] IETF, "The Atom Syndication Format."

[6] cf. Alby, "Web 2.0. Konzepte, Anwendungen, Technologien", 154

Hence Atom is the competitor of RSS to one single standardized format of web syndication.

2.4 BLOGS, BLOGGING AND BLOGOSPHERE

"A blog is a web page that contains brief, discrete blocks of information called posts. These posts are arranged in reverse-chronological order[...]. Each post is uniquely identified by an anchor tag, and it is marked with a permanent link that can be referred to by others[...]" [7]

Software developers introduced new techniques like permalinks or trackbacks to the Web 2.0 community and lead them to a prospering grow. Publishers of weblogs are known as bloggers and the whole environment of blogs and bloggers is the blogosphere.[8]

2.5 MICROBLOGGING AND TWITTER

Microblogging is a relatively new and fast growing technology to share thoughts, status and information. Mobile users can publish their information with the aid of internet connected mobile devices like cell phones, Personal Digital Assistants (PDAs) or even notebooks. The length of is typically between 130 and 200 characters per message.[9]

"Text messages are uploaded to a microblogging service such as Twitter[10], Jaiku[11] and others, and then distributed to group members."[12]

The main differences to the standard blogging are the frequency and length of the posts. Microblogging posts are restricted in length and updated much faster than regular blogs. A "normal" blogger will update his or her blog once every couple of days. Microbloggers will send several updates to their microblog(s) every day.

---

[7] Doctorow, Powers, and Trott, Essential Blogging.

[8] cf. Alby, "Web 2.0. Konzepte, Anwendungen, Technologien"

[9] Ibid.

[10] cf. "Twitter: What are you doing?."

[11] cf. "Jaiku | Your Conversation."

[12] "What is Microblogging?."

3 BACKGROUND

3.1 HISTORY

The following section gives a short overview about the development history of the two content delivery formats, RSS and Atom and their dispartment from one single standard. Most of this section is taken from Hammersley.[13]

3.1.1 META CONTENT FORMAT (MCF) AND RESOURCE DESCRIPTION FORMAT (RDF)

The first steps to RSS were made by the software developer Ramanathan V. Guha and his invention of the MCF. This Meta Content Framework was driven by the need of a standardized framework which was able to describe objects with attributes and linking them together in relationships. At Netscape Guha and Tim Bray transformed the MCF to an XML based format which grew up to become the RDF project.[14]

In its fullest form it is the basis of the Semantic Web, where *"computers can understand the meaning of, and the relationships between, documents and other data."*[15]

3.1.2 CHANNEL DEFINITION FORMAT (CDF)

Microsoft followed the development of XML based content description formats with its CDF. It was released in March 1997 and submitted to the W3C shortly after.[16]

The language is able to characterize the content of a web page, as well as a "sites particular rating, scheduling, logos and metadata."[17]

3.2 RSS

The first fully RDF – based format, RSS 0.9, was published in April 2001 by Dan Libby as an acronym for *RDF Site Summary.*[18]

RSS 0.91 was brought to the market three days later and created a trend for the future. It was not RDF – based and therefore not compatible to the first specification.

---

[13] Hammersley, "Developing Feeds with RSS and Atom", p. 2-10.

[14] cf. "Resource Description Framework (RDF) / W3C Semantic Web Activity."

[15] Hammersley, "Developing Feeds with RSS and Atom", p. 3.

[16] cf. "Channel Definition Format Submission 970309."

[17] Hammersley, "Developing Feeds with RSS and Atom", p. 3.

[18] cf. "Resource Description Framework (RDF) / W3C Semantic Web Activity."

The release of version 1.0 on December 6, 2000 was the fallback to an RDF – based data model with a high complexity.

Two weeks later, Dave Winer from UserLand Software released the 0.92 version, an alternative to the RDF based versions (0.9 and 1.0).

After the release of RSS 2.0 on September 16, 2002 UserLand declared the standard as frozen and without further developing possibilities.

On July 15, 2003 UserLand gave the copyrights to Harvard and they published it under the Creative Commons Attribution / Share Alike Licence. It is assured that version 0.9 and 0.91 are also valid 2.0 files.[19]

To sum up, the standard is forked but both are basing on the XML standard of W3C[20] and are extensible with own created namespaces, modules or containers.

3.3 ATOM

Atom addressed the shortcomings of RSS and quickly widespread after the release of Atom 0.3. An early adopter was Google with the implementation in services such as Gmail and Google News.

In August 2005 an independent group of webloggers suggested the Atom 1.0 format to the IETF. It was approved and published in the RFC 4287 document, as Proposed Standard.[21]

4 SOFTWARE

4.1 ONLINE OR OFFLINE

It is a determining question whether the approach should be online available and therefore follow the thoughts of 'cloud computing' or whether a desktop based solution would still be enough. Software vendors offer many different approaches of feed readers and even feed aggregators addressing the different needs. The single

---

[19] cf. "RSS 2.0 Specification (RSS 2.0 at Harvard Law)."

[20] cf. "Extensible Markup Language (XML) 1.0 (Fifth Edition)."

[21] IETF, "The Atom Syndication Format."

solutions comprise advantages and disadvantages and of course it is also a question of personal preferences.

4.1.1 ONLINE

Online applications take advantage of a software already existing on nearly every computer, the web-browser. Features like history, bookmarks and search are already implemented. Modern web applications emulate the behaviour of desktop solutions and provide an accustomed environment to the user, with the advantages of relatively easy maintenance and platform independence.

The process of feed reading is closely bound to a permanent internet connection.

This is surely a downside but in times of internet flatrates and mobile access a minor issue.

The user might want to read a full article of a feed excerpt, even if locally cached he has to switch between feed reader and web browser to follow included links, commenting on entries, streaming video or audio files.

In a web-based solution you just open another tab to receive the external data.

To assure the collaborative requirement, online applications early began to offer communities for thought sharing, connecting and networking.

4.1.2 OFFLINE

On the other hand desktop applications offer a responsive interface and fast data processing. Feeds can be stored locally an accessed everywhere e.g. in a plane or train.

You do not have to develop a very complex online web structure with a user concept, enough hard disk space to store all personal information and guaranteed access to the feed lists.

The platform dependence burdened the project with a higher workload for maintenance and development in the initial phase. To work around the platform dependence issue you can use JAVA, but the applications tend to an unresponsive interface.

Platform dependence comprise the necessity of synchronization, such as current 'read-status' or comments.

4.2 CONCLUSION

The feed reader should be web-based due to some advantages compared to a single desktop-based solution:

- It is platform independent and can be accessed with all types of web browsers.
- It provides a central data storage like personalized views, user data, additional metadata for the feeds and their entries.
- It enriches the platform with a collaborative background for user interaction and recommendation of information.

4.3 COMPETITIVE ANALYSES

As mentioned above the 'nice-to-have' feed reader is web-based and the following section will perform a small market analyse of already utilized feed readers.

The focus lays on collaborative features and their arrangement in the web browser. It does not provide a full overview of the whole online feed reader market likewise desktop-based solutions are out of scope.

4.3.1 GOOGLE READER

Google Reader is the feed syndication approach from Google, one of the biggest suppliers of web-based software. It also offers some collaborative features like flagging articles, same as favourites in a web browser, recommending articles and publishing comments – see figure beside.[22]

figure 2: Google Reader

To keep the overview about all subscriptions they also created a trend submenu to see how often the feeds were updated by the syndicator and how many posts you have read in the past and other useful statistical evaluations. To round off the collaborative software they enabled the user to share their feeds and recommend them to others.

4.3.2 NEWSGATOR

Newsgator is a fast growing software producer providing solutions for information management, desktop based software and furthermore web based clients to improve productivity.[23]

---

[22] "Google Reader."

[23] "NewsGator - Enterprise Social Computing via Social Sites on SharePoint, RSS and Widgets."

They offer also a syndication approach with collaborative enrichments like evaluation and video sharing. Most of the features are already established, like subscribing to a feed or tagging them. The feeds are organized in a tree structure with free definable folders. A unique feature is the videocast sharing. You can see videos added today and view them in the web browser. One competitive advantage is the online accessibility of the web based solution via smart phones or PDA's.

figure 3: videocast and tag cloud

Those two competitors show a small extract of the fast growing and innovative RSS / Atom reader market. Plenty software tools are available and some were tested shortly but I will not mention their features at length because they overlap in their features. See the list beneath to get a small overview:

- Attensa Online
- Bloglines
- GritWire
- News Alloy
- Rojo

It has shown that collaborative approaches are implemented sporadically but growing and becoming more professional.

Algorithms for automatic user evaluation and collaborative filtering are implemented as well as user interactive recommendation and multimedia information sharing.[24]

5 BLUEPRINT OF A COLLABORATIVE FEED READER

The software evaluation and literature research helped to divide between necessary and unnecessary features for one goal; efficient feed reading.

A research group published a comprehensive research about RSS usage and features[25]. New concepts based upon RSS were described in a paper of Prof. Peter

---

[24] Lemire and MacLachlan, "Slope on predictors for Online Rating-Based Collaborative Filtering."

[25] cf. Liu and Ram, "Client Behavior and Feed Characteristics of RSS, a Publish-Subscribe System for Web Mircronews."

Reusch.[26] The systematic overview at techchrunch.com was a good orientation about necessary features of web based feed readers.[27]

Due to a lack of scientifically information sources, most of the features are based on my own opinion.

5.1 GRAPHICAL USER INTERFACE (GUI)

For fast access to the required information it is very important that the GUI is clean and without any unnecessary features and easy to use. My approach is structured as follows.

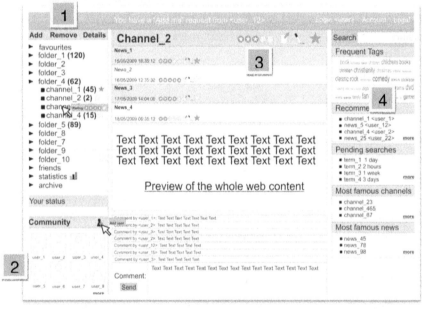

figure 4: Draft collaborative feed reader

5.1.1 SUBSCRIPTION LISTS

The base is a panel, see figure 4 green box number one, with features for feed consumption, editing and archiving in a tree structure.

---

[26] cf. Reusch, "New Communication Concepts based upon advanced RSS Feeds."

[27] cf. Gruber, "The State of Online Feed Readers."

Favourite feeds will be shared with your public network and statistical evaluations (bar graph) help you to optimize your information consumption.

5.1.2 COMMUNITY

The social network (box two) stays behind the collaborative approach for efficient news reading but it will not replace social networking software like Facebook or Xing. Establishing groups of added users ease the dedicate share of subscription lists and favourites. Like common in microbloggs, you can share your thoughts and activities with your network, keeping them up-to-date.

5.1.3 PREVIEW

A chosen feed is displayed in panel number three with details like feed name, feed entries and beneath a commentator section to discuss the entries.

Each feed and feed entry can be evaluated with the five displayed stars and furthermore recommended to other users with the white paper and orange arrow symbol.

The small pen symbolises the tagging feature of the approach to categorize it later on. The star beside is again the possibility to mark favourites.

5.1.4 SEARCHING FEEDS

The last panel is an aid to access new feed sources.

The search of new feeds and a Tag Cloud for topic specific access are used as well as recommended feeds and pending search queries to stay up-to-date with published items.

Furthermore you have a fast access to the most famous sources of the community and as is customary in web portals you can login, logout and access and change your private settings.

5.2 EVALUATION

5.2.1 AVERAGE RATING

The user evaluates feeds as well as individual feed entries with a 0 – 5 rating, whereas 0 being the worst and 5 the best rating.

The single rating values are added and divided by the count of ratings and displayed near the detailed feed and feed entry information.

5.2.2 SUBSCRIPTION COUNT

An additional method to evaluate feeds is the simply count how many people have subscribed a feed. The more have subscribed in the higher rated position you get in displaying the results of a search query. To keep track with changing trends you could additionally count how many users have subscribed or unsubscribed during a 7-day or 14-day period in a feed.

5.2.3 FAVOURITE

Favourite rankings are already implemented in web browsers like Mozilla Firefox and extensively used at delicious.com.

Linking collaborative filtering methods and bookmark popularity ratings with each other is a strong prediction method of information demand and preferences.[28]

This concept also helps gaining places in the most interesting feed lists and queries.

5.2.4 COVERAGE PERCENTAGE

The Coverage Percentage is a concept newly used in the IBM CoffeeReader. This feed reader is a collaborative news aggregator which enriches a normal feed reader by a social component.[29]

figure 5: IBM CoffeeReader

---

[28] Markines, Stoilova, and Menczer, "Bookmark Hierarchies and Collaborative Recommendation."

[29] cf. "IBM R&D Labs in Israel | CoffeeReader - Collaborative Feed Reader."

As shown in the image above, the feeds are rated with a coverage rate in percent. This rate shows a subscribed user how many posts from all published ones were read in the past and he can decide if he wants to follow further or cancel his subscription.

Moderators, creators or even administrators can see how often the posts were read in the past and by whom. With that knowledge they are able to change the content of the posts or the amount of posts per day to address their target group.

All these evaluation methods lead to one single goal, the efficient news consumption with the aim of social networks and collective intelligence and preferences.

5.3 COLLABORATIVE FILTERING

Two main models of rating prediction have been established in modern research papers: one is model based and the other one memory based.

On the one hand similarity between two users is used by memory based prediction algorithms and represented by a weighted average. E.g. User 1 and User 2 are neighbours by subscribing the news channel A, so when User 2 subscribes to channel Z it might be also interesting for User 1. Small implementation tests have shown that this statistical method only works with an extensive data set and beforehand acquired information about the users.

On the other hand model based algorithms link items together and create a matrix with the relationships between them. E.g.: channel 1 is related to channel 2, therefore can a user, who is reading channel 1 also be interested in reading channel 2.[30]

Both methods ailing with the so-called 'ramp-up' or 'cold-start' problem. If the system does not know any preferences of new users or also evaluations of new feeds, the system fails in precise prediction. Hence a combination of several algorithms is necessary to deal with the 'ramp-up' problem.[31]

One of the most famous hybrid prediction algorithms is utilized by Amazon, see figure beneath and named 'item-to-item collaborative filtering'. It separates the process into an online and offline sub-process. The offline process is utilized to compute the similarities between the single feeds and the storage in a 'similar-to-item' table.

---

[30]cf. Breese, Heckerman, and Kadie, "Empirical Analysis of Predictive Algorithms for Collaborative Filtering."

[31] cf. Burke, "Hybrid Recommender Systems: Survey and Experiments."

Whereas the online process combines user information and recommended or viewed items with each other to display potential interesting items to the user.[32]

This algorithm can be adopted for feed prediction as well by substitution the items by feeds or even feed entries and pre-processing the 'feed-to-feed similarity table' offline.

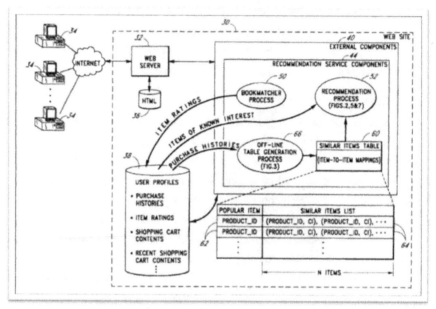

figure 6: Item-to-Item Collaborative Filtering from Amazon[33]

5.4 SUPPORTED FORMATS

Presently there are more than 9 versions of feed formats spread on the market. However, most of them are not compatible with the other versions.

"RSS 0.90 is incompatible with Netscape's RSS 0.91, Netscape's RSS 0.91 is incompatible with Userland's RSS 0.91, Netscape's RSS 0.91 is incompatible with RSS 1.0, Userland's RSS 0.91 is incompatible with RSS 0.92, RSS 0.92 is incompatible with RSS 0.93, RSS 0.93 is incompatible with RSS 0.94, RSS 0.94 is incompatible with RSS 2.0, and RSS 2.0 is incompatible with itself."[34]

---

[32] Linden, Smith, and York, "Amazon.com Recommendations: Item-to-Item Collaborative Filtering."

[33] cf. Stock, "Information Retrieval: Informationen suchen und finden."

[34] "The myth of RSS compatibility [dive into mark]."

Furthermore two Atom formats can be found today, the versions 1.0 and 0.3. You have to synchronise approximately 11 feed formats with each other and make them accessible to the user. Hence you need an additional XML format changing language.

5.5 XLS TRANSFORMATION

The usage of the XSL Transformation format is a good step to an appropriate solution.[35] It describes a language to transform XML documents into other XML, text or binary based documents. Below (figure seven) you can view a simplified XSLT transformation process to create a new XML document.

The process 'translates' XML source documents with the aid of XSLT code templates and the XLST processor to outbound documents.

Villard and Lyaida created an exemplary transformation process. The entry document is XML-based and organized in a tree structure. Beside you can see the XSLT template with references of HTML and links to the source and outbound document. They create a HTML website out of a XML document.[36]

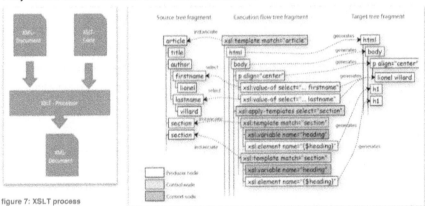

figure 7: XSLT process

figure 8: Exemplary XSLT process

With this you are able to create a standardized XML or HTML document which you can display in your GUI. It has advantages in creating your own document structure no matter in which feed the user had subscribed in and which format (Atom/RSS) the feed uses.

---

[35] cf. "XSL Transformations (XSLT) Version 2.0."

[36] cf. Villard and Lyaida, "XSLT Transformation," 5.

5.6 TAGGING

Tagging is one of the new buzzwords in the Web 2.0 community. A tag is some form of metadata information about a content added automatically by algorithms or users. Tags are not hierarchically organised and based on the theory of Ontology.[37]

The algorithms can support the user by choosing appropriate tags. One opportunity to suggest tags for a feed or a feed entry is crawling through the whole feed, Text Mining and the related web content and displaying the three most frequent terms. [38]

This strategy is not the most efficient one because the most frequent terms will mostly be words without any significance for content like 'the', 'I' or 'and'. There are many possibilities to implement algorithms, which are, however, not to be discussed in this paper.

For further information see, among other things *"Personalized, Interactive Tag Recommendation for Flickr"*.[39]

Another possibility is the tagging by a single or a group of users. Everybody can suggest one or more keywords, which identifies the feed or feed entry most suitable. These tags can be used as search criteria in a search engine or can be displayed in a tag cloud in the interface. A combination of automated Text Mining algorithms and manual user tagging is the best approach.

5.7 TAG CLOUD

"Tag clouds are visual displays of set of words (or 'tags') in which attributes of the text such as size, color or font weight are used to represent relevant properties e.g. frequency of documents linked to the tag."[40]

Tag clouds help users to get fast access to the content of a web page or a certain area. But tag clouds and their use are controversially discussed. On the one hand they provide the user with a fast overview about most recent terms and expressions of the web content, on the other hand the size of buzzwords and the length can be

---

[37] cf. Gruber, "Ontology of Folksonomy."

[38] cf. Dörre, Gerstl, and Seiffert, "Text Mining: Finding Nuggets in Mountains of Textual Data."

[39] cf. Garg and Weber, "Personalized, Interactive Tag Recommendation for Flickr."

[40] Schrammel, Leitner, and Tscheligi, "Semantically Structured Tag Clouds: An Empirical Evaluation of Clustered Presentation Approaches."

irritating. A research group from CURE - Center for Usability Research and Engineering in Vienna[41] and Marti A. Hearst and Daniela Rosner from the University of California, Berkeley[42] have made studies about the usage of tag clouds.

figure 9: Tag cloud from Amazon.com

One research result is that tagging and tag clouds are a good possibility to give the user a fast access to the information and the related content. However, the usability can be further improved by evaluations about tags and ratings as well as automatic extraction by Text Mining tools. The increasing occurrence of recent terms should be ranked higher than older buzzwords.

One example of a tag cloud is seen on the left with popular keywords enlarged.

5.8 EXPORT AND IMPORT

The ideal collaborative feed reader has an import and export functionality for the subscription lists.

Some approaches offer the Outline Processor Markup Language (OPML) to support the user by switching the already used tool and managing the feed lists. No user want to enter all subscribed feed hyperlinks again in another tool.

5.9 OPML FORMAT

The 'Outline Processor Markup Language' stores outlines in XML 1.0 format. This format is hierarchically structured and therefore perfectly eligible for exporting and importing feed lists.[43]

This feature is very crucial for sharing your subscribed feeds with others or for archiving purposes.

---

[41] Ibid.

[42] cf. Hearst and Rosner, "Tag Clouds: Data Analysis Tool or Social Signaller?."

[43] cf. "OPML 1.0 Specification."

5.10 COMMUNITY

To satisfy the requirement as a collaborative tool you should establish an active wide spread community within the approach. Communities are a good possibility to share information between peers and non-peers.

But there should not be any information overflow. A picture of the user, main interests, free time activities, address, chat accounts and some other personal information in a text field should be enough. The community is a special way to share as private marked information or feeds among each other.

Like seen above this is important to make meaningful suggestions of feeds to other users in the community.

5.11 PODCASTS / VIDEO PODCASTS

The amazing success of You Tube and last.fm has shown that the demand for multimedia is unbroken and growing rapidly.

A (video) podcast is a (video) radio broadcast and mostly published without any fees by the author, delivered via feeds. Figure ten shows a logo indicating podcast subscriptions. They can be distributed as downloadable file or as stream. The approach should be aware of this possibility with a separate media player, like iTunes, Windows Media Player or VLC to play the delivered media file or stream and to enrich the reader approach with a multimedia aspect.

figure 10: unofficial podcast logo

5.12 SEARCH / SEARCH AGENT

It is very hard to browse through the huge amount of news feeds published in the internet nowadays.

The search with the word "rss" delivers 1,688,517 indexed feeds in all languages across all channels at technorati.[44] That is a possibly unable to browse through amount of information.

Google alerts users automatically when new content is published in a predefined search query.[45]

[44] cf. "Technorati Search: rss."

[45] cf. "Google Alerts Help."

The search functionality provides the user with a search agent for periodical updates of new feeds. Additionally you can define the frequency how often the search engine should perform your request.

The search feature should also be able to crawl through all indexed feeds and tags and deliver the results at once. Therefore you need an efficient search algorithm which enables you to weight the value of a tag, number of found hits in the text, evaluation results (as defined above) and more to display the most suitable feeds on the top of the result query.

5.13 ARCHIVE

You cannot rely on permanent stored content in the World Wide Web. Hence you need a separate storage solution for your web-portal. It is a possibility for users to store single feed entries or even whole feeds to read them later or due to research activities.

Some web-pages like weblogs or news pages are going to use permalinks as steady link to the content. A permalink is still usable when the weblog was deleted or the page is archived in a big storage.[46]

The content can be stored as XML files in a database and if the user wants also with all linked files of the feed entry e.g. Podcast files, web pages or pictures. But this option should be reconsidered twice because you need significantly more storage capacity whereas some media could be stored with a permalink. The data behind this permalink does not need to be stored, since it is meant to be available permanently; as far as that can go on the internet.

6 CONCLUSION

Feeds are a fast growing and still very innovative concept for information sharing and user interaction.

To reach a big community you have to communicate the aim of feeds and you should try to reduce the fear about this new technology. The aggregator approaches must be easy to use and support the user during the information lifecycle process.

---

[46] cf. Alby, "Web 2.0. Konzepte, Anwendungen, Technologien",p. 246

Andreas Schneider evaluated XWiki Watch in his paper "The case of XWiki Watch" giving a short appraisal of the implemented features as well as a small list of possible improvements.

Seeing that present approaches support the user by handling the information overflow but they must be further improved with collaborative features like evaluation methods, recommendation features and communities.

The drafted solution is a good possibility to enhance the productivity of single users as well as groups in a complex interaction process. Implementing and combination already existing elements of different approaches in various fields e.g. shopping prediction, feed reader, blogs/microblogs or social networking software should be used primarily – like tagging, social interaction via communities, feeds organised in a tree structure and collaborative filtering and predicting.

Multimedia content reached a higher importance in everyday communication and social interaction. The solution should be aware of a fast growing and innovative multimedia market and thus open for further developments.

This approach is a good opportunity to handle the growing information overflow.

Bibliography

Alby, Tom. "Web 2.0. Konzepte, Anwendungen, Technologien". 1st ed. Hanser Fachbuchverlag, 2008.

Breese, John S., David Heckerman, and Carl Kadie. "Empirical Analysis of Predictive Algorithms for Collaborative Filtering," May 1998. http://web.mate.polimi.it/seminari_cm/seminari/file/tom1(1).pdf.

Burke, Robin. "Hybrid Recommender Systems: Survey and Experiments." http://www.cs.pitt.edu/~mrotaru/comp/rs/Burke%20UMUAI%202002.pdf.

"Channel Definition Format Submission 970309." http://www.w3.org/TR/NOTE-CDFsubmit.html.

Doctorow, Cory, Shelley Powers, and Mena G. Trott. *Essential Blogging*. O'Reilly Media, 2002.

Dörre, Jochen, Peter Gerstl, and Roland Seiffert. "Text Mining: Finding Nuggets in Mountains of Textual Data," 1999. http://www.cs.uvm.edu/~xwu/kdd/KDD-dorre.pdf.

"Extensible Markup Language (XML) 1.0 (Fifth Edition)." http://www.w3.org/TR/xml/.

Garg, Nikhil, and Ingmar Weber. "Personalized, Interactive Tag Recommendation for Flickr," 2008. http://delivery.acm.org/10.1145/1460000/1454020/p67-garg.pdf?key1=1454020&key2=4338730421&coll=Portal&dl=GUIDE&CFID=32248009&CFTOKEN=61792829.

"Google Alerts Help." http://www.google.com/support/alerts/#q1.

"Google Reader." http://www.google.de/reader/view/#overview-page.

Gruber, Frank. "The State of Online Feed Readers," March 30, 2006. http://www.techcrunch.com/2006/03/30/the-state-of-online-feed-readers/.

Gruber, Thomas. "Ontology of Folksonomy," 2007. http://tomgruber.org/writing/ontology-of-folksonomy.htm.

Hammersley, Ben. "Developing Feeds with RSS and Atom". O'Reilly Media, Inc., 2005.

Hearst, Marti A., and Daniela Rosner. "Tag Clouds: Data Analysis Tool or Social Signaller?." *Tag Clouds: Data Analysis Tool or Social Signaller?* http://www2.computer.org/plugins/dl/pdf/proceedings/hicss/2008/3075/00/30750160.pdf?template=1&loginState=1&userData=anonymous-IP%253A%253A127.0.0.1.

Hoguhton-Jan, Sarah. "Being Wired or Being Tired - 10 Ways to Cope with Information Overload."

http://www.amok.am/tmp/Being%20Wired%20or%20Being%20Tired%20-
%2010%20Ways%20to%20Cope%20with%20Information%20Overload.pdf.

"IBM R&D Labs in Israel | CoffeeReader - Collaborative Feed Reader."
http://www.haifa.ibm.com/projects/imt/coffeereader/index.shtml.

IETF. "The Atom Syndication Format."
http://www.ietf.org/rfc/rfc4287.txt.

"Jaiku | Your Conversation." http://www.jaiku.com/.

Lemire, Daniel, and Anna MacLachlan. "Slope on predictors for Online Rating-Based
Collaborative Filtering," May 7, 2005. http://www.daniel-
lemire.com/fr/documents/publications/lemiremaclachlan_sdm05.pdf.

Linden, Greg, Brent Smith, and Yeremy York. "Amazon.com Recommendations:
Item-to-Item Collaborative Filtering," 3, 2003.
http://www.cs.umd.edu/~samir/498/Amazon-Recommendations.pdf.

Liu, and Ram. "Client Behavior and Feed Characteristics of RSS, a Publish-
Subscribe System for Web Mircronews."
http://www.cs.cornell.edu/people/egs/papers/rsssurvey.pdf.

Liu, Hongzhou, Venugopalan Ramasubramanian, and Emin Gun Sirer. "Client
Behavior and Feed Characteristics of RSS, a Publish-Subscribe System for
Web Micronews." http://www.cs.cornell.edu/people/egs/papers/rsssurvey.pdf.

Markines, Ben, Lubomira Stoilova, and Filippo Menczer. "Bookmark Hierarchies and
Collaborative Recommendation," 2006.

"NewsGator - Enterprise Social Computing via Social Sites on SharePoint, RSS and
Widgets." http://www.newsgator.com/.

"OPML 1.0 Specification." http://www.opml.org/spec.

Reusch, Peter J.A. Reusch. "New Communication Concepts based upon advanced
RSS Feeds," 2004. http://www.fh-
dortmund.de/de/ftransfer/medien/reusch2.pdf.

"Resource Description Framework (RDF) / W3C Semantic Web Activity."
http://www.w3.org/RDF/.

"RSS 2.0 Specification (RSS 2.0 at Harvard Law)."
http://cyber.law.harvard.edu/rss/rss.html.

Schrammel, Johann, Michael Leitner, and Manfred Tscheligi. "Semantically
Structured Tag Clouds: An Empirical Evaluation of Clustered Presentation
Approaches," April 9, 2009.
http://delivery.acm.org/10.1145/1520000/1519010/p2037-
schrammel.pdf?key1=1519010&key2=5759730421&coll=Portal&dl=GUIDE&C
FID=32248009&CFTOKEN=61792829.

Stock, Wolfgang G. "Information Retrieval: Informationen suchen und finden," 2007. http://www.amazon.de/Information-Retrieval-Informationen-suchen-finden/dp/3486581724/ref=sr_1_1?ie=UTF8&s=books&qid=1243005069&sr=8-1.

"Technorati Search: rss." http://technorati.com/search/rss?language=n&authority=n.

"The myth of RSS compatibility [dive into mark]." http://diveintomark.org/archives/2004/02/04/incompatible-rss.

"Twitter: What are you doing?." http://twitter.com/.

Villard, Lionel, and Nabil Lyaida. "An incremental XSLT Transformation Processor for XML Data Maniupulation," May 11, 2002.

"What is Microblogging?." http://www.wisegeek.com/what-is-microblogging.htm.

"XSL Transformations (XSLT) Version 2.0." http://www.w3.org/TR/xslt20/#xslt-mime-definition.

Bibligraphy of figures

figure 1: rss graphics in accordance to www.rss-specifications.com

"http://www.rss-specifications.com/rss-graphics.htm", May 10, 2009.

figure 2: Google Reader

"http://www.google.com/reader/view/", May 08, 2009.

figure 3: videocast and tag cloud

"http://www.newsgator.com/ngs/subscriber/WebEd2.aspx", April 14, 2009.

figure 4: Draft collaborative feed reader

figure 5: IBM CoffeeReader

"http://www.haifa.ibm.com/projects/imt/coffeereader/index.shtml",
April 08, 2009.

figure 6: Item-to-Item Collaborative Filtering from Amazon.com

Stock, Wolfgang G. "Information Retrieval: Informationen suchen und finden",
2007.

figure 7: XSLT process

figure 8: Exemplary XSLT process

Villard, Lionel, and Nabil Lyaida. "An incremental XSLT Transformation
Processor for XML Data Maniupulation", p. 479, May 11, 2002.

figure 9: Tag cloud from Amazon.com

"http://www.amazon.com/gp/tagging/cloud/ref=tag_sr_nss?redirect=true",
April 01, 2009.

figure 10: unofficial podcast logo

"http://upload.wikimedia.org/wikipedia/commons/thumb/e/e1/Videopodcast_l
ogo.jpg/507px-Videopodcast_logo.jpg", April 10, 2009.

www.ingramcontent.com/pod-product-compliance
Lightning Source LLC
LaVergne TN
LVHW042309060326
832902LV00009B/1378